<u>Ultimate Guide to Manual Handling</u>
A Real World Approach

By Lee Marsh

Order this book online at www.trafford.com/07-2408
or email orders@trafford.com

Most Trafford titles are also available at major online book retailers.

Note for Librarians: A cataloguing record for this book is available from Library
and Archives Canada at www.collectionscanada.ca/amicus/index-e.html

Edited by Rachel Kelly

ISBN: 978-1-4251-5412-7

*We at Trafford believe that it is the responsibility of us all, as both individuals
and corporations, to make choices that are environmentally and socially sound.
You, in turn, are supporting this responsible conduct each time you purchase a
Trafford book, or make use of our publishing services. To find out how you are
helping, please visit www.trafford.com/responsiblepublishing.html*

*Our mission is to efficiently provide the world's finest, most comprehensive
book publishing service, enabling every author to experience success.
To find out how to publish your book, your way, and have it available
worldwide, visit us online at www.trafford.com/10510*

Trafford
PUBLISHING™

www.trafford.com

North America & international
toll-free: 1 888 232 4444 (USA & Canada)
phone: 250 383 6864 ♦ fax: 250 383 6804
email: info@trafford.com

The United Kingdom & Europe
phone: +44 (0)1865 722 113 ♦ local rate: 0845 230 9601
facsimile: +44 (0)1865 722 868 ♦ email: info.uk@trafford.com

10 9 8 7 6 5 4 3 2 1

Contents

Part 3 – Managing and Supervising

Part 4 – Reference Section

4

I must say a big thank you to Joanne, Becky, Sue and Rachel for all their help and support in getting this book ready.

Preface

Lee Marsh is one of Risk Management and Health & Safety's most hidden gems, specifically where Manual Handling, Leadership in Safety, Walking the Talk and Real World Business Continuity Planning are concerned. His animated, action-packed style demands participation. In my years of attending, Risk and Safety presentations and training events, I have never seen so much audience involvement. Lee does not give his audience the option of sitting back and merely reflecting.

Having attended a manual-handling seminar being presented by Lee, I wondered how his presentation style would translate into words on pages and was delighted to find that the reader of this handbook is as bullied and cajoled into participation as is the listener!

The people to whom this handbook is directed, will be forced to look at their own manual handling and that of others, along with when and why the various methods are employed. Throughout, this handbook engages and holds the attention by finding practical solutions and maximising the benefits of manual handling issues for businesses and organisations alike.

If the first key characteristic of this handbook is its emphasis upon participation, the second is on simplicity. Lee Marsh emphasises that manual handling is not rocket science, but neither should the thought of manual handling effectively be underestimated. What he correctly stresses is that business owners, managers, supervisors and all employees have their own part to play when it comes to manual handling.

His background as a professional trainer and consultant for Health & Safety, Risk Management and Business Continuity Planning for businesses such as Wincanton Logistics, ASDA, and ICI Paints means that Lee's wealth of experience and expertise make a refreshing change. Rather than merely receiving the principles, this handbook offers practical advice and guidance in this particular subject area.

I also thought it was a great idea to use illustrations that Lee himself draws on whiteboards and flipcharts during training sessions when he is explaining specific information.

Louise Peters
CEO
Real World – Risk, Safety, Training & Projects

INTRODUCTION

Managing people and supervising activities of employees is one of the most challenging yet rewarding of all management tasks. Managers and supervisors have a high level of responsibility and are the catalyst for success in any organisation.

Success has many components. The most important factor is the overall performance of the employees. If they work together as a team, success comes easily. If, however one or two employees are not performing as required, the entire team fails. Workplace injuries, illness and absenteeism disrupt the performance of the work force, leading to a place of work where people no longer like working, these then lead to other issues such as; poor housekeeping, poor quality, more injuries, more sick days, loss of cash flow etc...

One problem, which has the potential to be very disruptive, is a back injury. An employee with a back injury is usually out of work for a good period of time and when they are able to return, usually require restrictions so called "light duties". It sometimes seems as though the injury never goes away and that the problem just continues to get worse. The good news is that there are positive steps which can be taken to reduce the likelihood, manage and perhaps even prevent.

"Ultimate Guide to Manual Handling" has been specifically written to help reduce, if not, prevent back injuries in, and outside of, the workplace. In Part 1 of this handbook, employees learn how the back works, the types and causes of back disorders and how to prevent and manage back problems. In Part 2, a number of different lifting techniques that can be applied and discussed. If they follow the principles that are presented they should be well on their way to having healthier backs. It is not always that easy so included in Part 3 is a session for managers. A good manager or supervisor can make a big difference by making sure that the principles and techniques taught are used on a daily basis.

This book provides solid information about body mechanics, workplace design and modification. Ultimate Guide to Manual Handling also covers management of claims costs and the importance of a positive return-to-work program. Through the implementation of these principles and programs, back injuries can be severely reduced if not prevented and ultimately managed more successfully.

Lee Marsh
Senior Consultant & Trainer
Real World – Risk, Safety, Training & Projects

Part 1

Understanding
Manual Handling

Part 1 – Understanding Manual Handling

1.1 - Just What is Manual Handling?

You can pick up any health and safety book and when you look up Manual Handling it is likely to give you a definition like "the movement of articles by the use of muscular strength, movement and body weight", but what does it mean? Well for the purpose of this book and for the purpose of risk assessment, I suggest that you don't include the manual handling activity of using a pen (I know there will be so called health and safety professionals wanting to lynch me for that comment). As individuals involved in manual handling, let us look at the areas of most concern, and see what we can do about them.

A quick question, where do you do most of your lifting and moving of items?

```
┌─────────────────────────────────────────────────────────┐
│                                                           │
│                                                           │
│                                                           │
│                                                           │
└─────────────────────────────────────────────────────────┘
```

Thinking out loud here, but you are likely to do a fair bit of lifting at home too, new furniture, gardening, going to the tip, lifting up your children or grand children etc… One thing we must all grasp early on is that most of us will build up our manual handling injuries everyday throughout our lives and that to keep us active and free of back problems we must apply the best manual handling principles to every manual handling activity-whether at work or at home.

Manual Handling involves:

Lifting
Lowering
Holding
Pushing
Pulling
Dragging

Take a few minutes to think of activities that you have done over the last 24 hours that have involved the following: (write your answers down next to the heading)

❑ Lifting:

❑ Lowering:

❑ Holding (for over 2 minutes)

❑ Pushing

❑ Pulling

❑ Dragging

Now think about which of these were work related and which were home activities? (highlight the work activities)

Manual Handling and You

As an introduction into the subject of manual handling it is important that you ask yourself the questions below. Have a read through the questions and answer them as honestly as your want, remember this is your book.

Start by asking yourself:

Is good manual handling important to me? If so, why?

Have you ever lifted an item poorly? If so, what was it? Why did you lift it? When did you do it?

Have you ever suffered pain or discomfort following a manual handling activity?

If you were to suffer from back pain for a short time, say 10 days, what are the impacts it would have on you? (Think about the activities you would not be able to do)

What impact would the above injury have on your family?

If you were to suffer chronic back pain for the rest of your life, what are the impacts it would have on your life?

1.2 - How Our Bodies Work Whilst We Work

To help you understand how manual handling effects us all, let us first take a look at the body and how it is constructed, how it works and how we damage it.

List here what you know about the spine:

The Spine: (label the diagrams, answers can be found in Part 4 of this book)

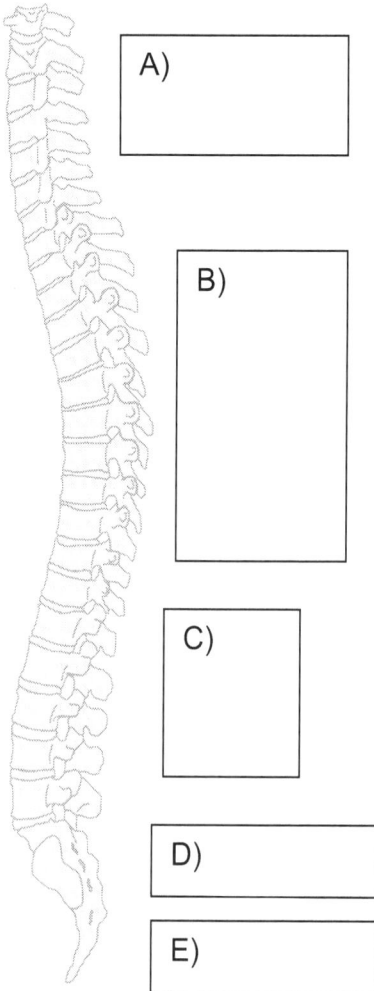

A)

B)

C)

D)

E)

Figure 1.1

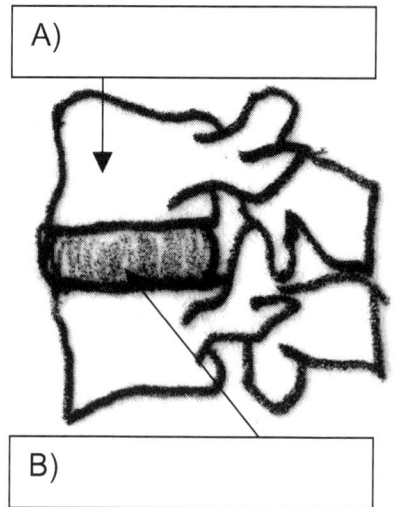

A)

B)

Figure 1.2

The spine, or spinal column, is the bony structure that makes up the backbone, supports the head, and provides a protective case for the spinal cord-the part of the central nervous system carrying messages between the brain and the rest of the body.

To allow us to stand vertically and to give us our range of movement, our spines have developed so that when viewed laterally (side on) it looks "S" shaped.

As you can see in figure 1.1 the spine is made up of a vertebrae column, and has 24 individual vertebrae, which are arranged into regions, the cervical (neck), thoracic (between your shoulders, where your ribs attach to the spine), and the lumbar (the base of the back, where we often feel discomfort); the sacral (back of the pelvis) and coocygeal (Tail bone) vertebrae are fused.

As most manual handling damage is cumulative, building up over a period of time, and generally in the lumbar region of the back, which we are going to focus a little bit more on it.

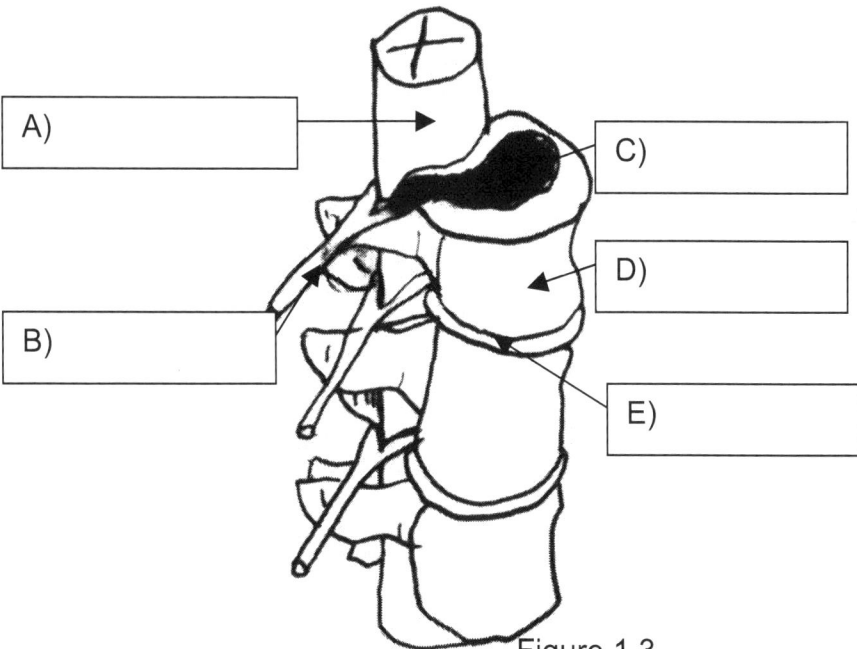

A)

B)

C)

D)

E)

Figure 1.3

Back pain usually starts in the lower back called the lumbar region. This part of our spine supports the mass of weight our upper body and head (3 to 4 Kg) produces, and it the most affected area for manual handling injuries.

The five lumbar vertebrae are the largest of all the vertebrae. Their thick processes secure the attachments of numerous ligaments and muscles/tendons, allowing us a good deal of movement and giving upper body support. The spinal cord terminates in the lumbar region of the spine.

Through natural wear and tear of our body, a large percentage of us are likely to have wearing of the discs between these vertebrate, which can be herniated, more often than not these herniated discs will press on nerves that splint off from the spinal cord causing inflammation, swelling, pain, stiffness in the muscles etc...

In many cases, these injuries will reduce (never fully go away) and from then on we will occasionally suffer with intermittent back pain. An evergrowing number of people however are suffering more traumatic back injuries, these herniated disks press on to and trap nerves such as the sciatic nerve, causing sometimes permanent pain in either or both legs. In some severe cases the herniated discs press on the spinal cord causing irreparable damage resulting in loss of motor control below that point.

Interestingly, you may have done this yourself. When you suffer back pain, you naturally move more gingerly and as a consequence we then tend to move in slow smooth actions, we bend our knees, and only lift that which is easy. What is really interesting here, are the mechanisms, when we hurt ourselves and have pain in our back we use all the right muscles and lift in a technically correct manner.

Question: As a child, at what age were you taught to lift?

The chances are you were never taught to lift, it just naturally happened. If you ever watch a young child lift, they generally lift the way we all should.

16

As we grow, our back muscles become strong, and for some strange reason we decide that lifting with these muscle seems easier and requires less effort. The strain on the lower back, however, is tremendous and increases the rate of natural wear and tear on our backs and, in most of us, on the discs that separate the vertebra which leads to herniated discs (see figure 1.3) - causing the aforementioned.

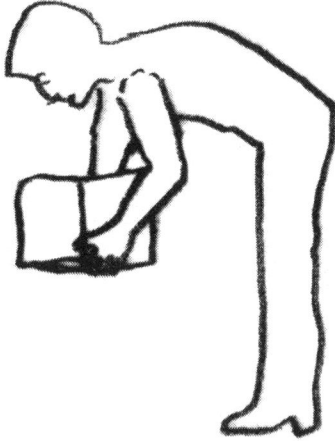

The heavier an item is, the greater the pressure on the lumbar region of the spine (see figure 1.4). Likewise the further away an object is from the core of the body the more pressure it exerts on the same region of the spine. This increase in pressure placed upon the spine can be more than five times the weight of the object.

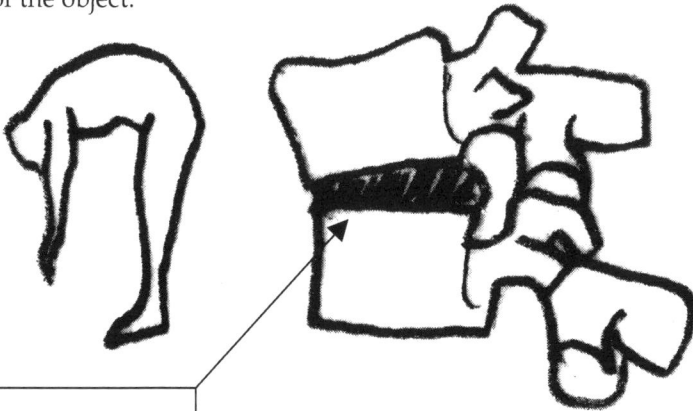

A)

Figure 1.4

There is light at the end of the tunnel, our leg muscles are used to support our body weight every day and they are the same muscles that children use when lifting (I am sure you can see where I am going with this). If, therefore we use our natural body mechanisms (for example, the leg muscles when lifting), we can reduce the strain placed on our backs. Remember our leg muscles are some of the strongest muscles in our bodies.

I feel it is important to stress that if individuals have not been lifting correctly with their legs, the initial attempts at lifting correctly feel a little strange. People often say to me that it does not feel comfortable however, after some practice and time spent lifting correctly, it is surprising that people start to find lifting correctly comfortable.

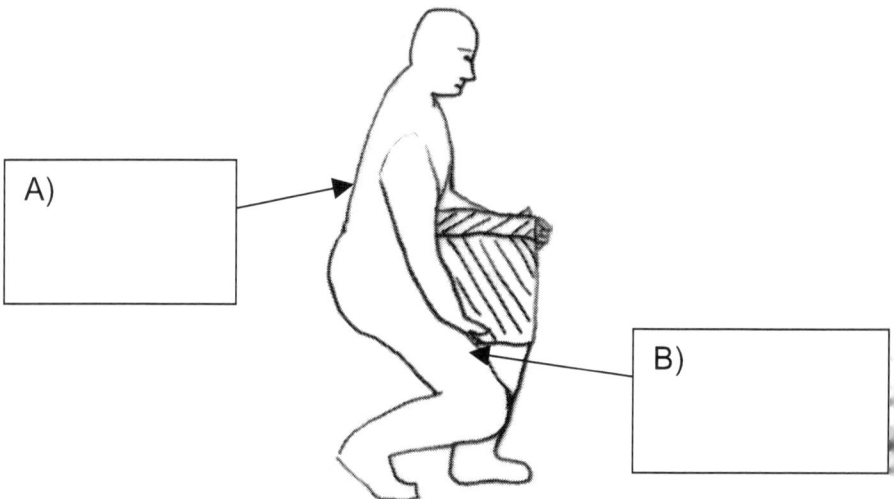

A)

B)

Figure 1.5

List here what might prevent you from lifting correctly:

```



```

Now think about why people should lift correctly:

```



```

What are the advantages for you to lift in a good manner?

```



```

What can you personally do to allow you to lift in the best possible way?

```



```

1.3 - The Back Problem

Back injuries could be called the plague of our adult population. Next to the common cold, a back injury is the reason most often cited for work sickness.

Back problems affect around 80% of the adult population in the United Kingdom, and can be directly linked to life style, stressful activities at home and at work, and to the overall level of our physical fitness.

Back pain results in 5 million workdays being lost annually, and accounts for one in five cases of work related ill health- the estimated NHS physiotherapy annual costs are estimated at £250.6 million. Back pain is the nation's leading cause of disability, with 1.1 million people disabled by it.

Most people believe that back injuries are the result of a lifting accident, or that something has slipped out of place and is causing pain. They also think that if there is a problem, they can go to the doctor, physiotherapist or chiropractor and have the problem fixed. **Wrong!**

Most back injuries are actually caused by the cumulative effect of the things we do every day. Incorrect standing or sitting posture, improper body mechanics and movements, staying in one position for too long, being overweight or under prolonged physical stress, and not maintaining muscle strength and flexibility all add up over time.

Managers and supervisors can influence many of these cumulative factors by supporting a manual handling good practice program. It is important that those in managerial positions establish safe work rules and performance standards, and then make certain they are followed by leading by example, never turning a blind eye to poor practices- in essence "Walking the Talk".

Businesses may not be able to enforce that employees exercise so that they are in good physical shape, but they can require them to stretch before performing handling tasks. They can also supervise to ensure the use of proper manual handling techniques, work with the employees to design jobs with safety in mind and require the use of lifting aids and devices or specify team lifting of heavy objects.

Any manager, supervisor or team leader in a workplace where manual handling tasks are performed is likely to encounter employees with back injuries. The Ultimate Guide to Manual Handling presents specific ideas about how to prevent the problem from affecting the workforce performance.

1.4 - Preventing Back Injuries

Trying to prevent back injuries is very difficult if you do not truly understand how they happen and what things increase the chance of them occurring.

Firstly make a list of the things you feel are the causes of back pain/injuries:

With these factors in mind, write down what you feel employees can do to prevent back injuries:

```
┌─────────────────────────────────────────────────────────────────┐
│                                                                   │
│                                                                   │
│                                                                   │
│                                                                   │
│                                                                   │
└─────────────────────────────────────────────────────────────────┘
```

Now let us think about what employers, managers and supervisors can do to help in preventing back injuries:

```
┌─────────────────────────────────────────────────────────────────┐
│                                                                   │
│                                                                   │
│                                                                   │
│                                                                   │
│                                                                   │
└─────────────────────────────────────────────────────────────────┘
```

Back injuries almost always result from the cumulative effect of five major factors:

1. Poor Posture – how we sit, how we stand and how we move.
2. Our Body Mechanics – how we lift, hold, push, pull or move objects.
3. How we carry out tasks – staying in one position for too long or not learning to relax.
4. Loss of Flexibility – becoming stiff and unable to utilise the full range of the body's movement capabilities.
5. Physical Fitness – loss of strength and endurance necessary to perform physical tasks without strain.

Generally speaking, there are four methods for prevention:

1. Workplace design and/or modification – eliminate the task or make the job less stressful.
2. Good lifting techniques – train and instruct employees to use good handling techniques and supervise the implementation.
3. Rotation of difficult activities – allow workers to change positions frequently, space stressful tasks throughout the day and utilise team-lifting techniques.
4. Make sure employees are physically capable – encourage employees to maintain an acceptable level of fitness.

Training employees in the safe ways to lift will have a significant long-term impact on back injury prevention and reduce sick days taken due to manual handling malpractice. Though it is true that physically stressful tasks and prolonged body positions can be reduced and in some cases even eliminated through proper workplace design, it is important that you remember that back injuries caused off the job also result in a high number of lost work days.

Over the years I have found that changing people's beliefs about manual handling, and seeing when, why, how and what they have lifted poorly is just as important as instructing people how to lift correctly now, otherwise the training is short lived. Over the years I have created a number of manual handling packages for clients and businesses that I have worked for, and into all of these I have built a strong emphasis on long term changes, focusing on beliefs and behaviours.

Belief and Behaviour

Many trainers, consultants and managers try to change the way people work by focusing on behaviours. They keep thinking they can make things better by doing something and then try to figure out what it is they can do. The focus is on doing something, rather than on believing something.

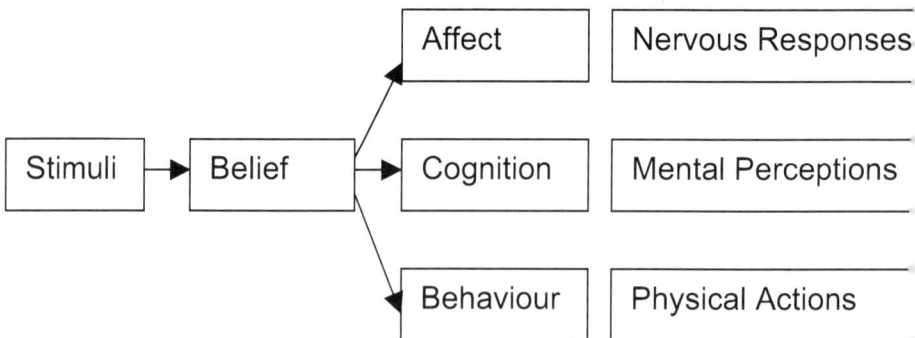

Stimuli	Belief	Affect	Nervous Responses
		Cognition	Mental Perceptions
		Behaviour	Physical Actions

Beliefs represent the knowledge of information we have about our environment (even though they may be inaccurate or not process all the information). Over the years in Health & Safety Training I have found that to convert a belief into an attitude, a valuable ingredient is needed which, by necessity, is related to an individuals sense of what is desirable, good, worthwhile, valuable etc…

In essence, belief can be simply put as:

$$\textbf{Belief} = \text{Expectancy} \times \text{Value}$$

Throughout history, forces within our societies have always sought to change things by using the power of thought then of action, for they know that mental thought produces physical action. Get a person thinking a certain way and you can get a person to act a certain way. It is not easily done the other way around.

Take killing, for example. You can rarely get a person to go out and kill another person simply by telling him to do so. You have to give him a reason. 'Reason' exists only in thought and thought is always based on Belief. So, if you want get one person to kill another, the fastest way to do that is to give him a belief that supports the action, and can sponsor it. While most of the world is seeking to bring about change by telling people what to DO, those who truly know how to motivate people are bringing about changes by telling them what to BELIEVE.

You can take whatever action you want to take to alter someone else's behaviour or to stop it, but unless you alter the beliefs that produced such behaviour, you will affect no changes, alter nothing and stop nothing. You can alter belief in two ways. Either, by enlarging upon it, or by changing it completely. But you must do one or the other or you will not alter behaviour. You will merely interrupt it.

Write down here when your behaviour had changed, but eventually went back to what it was previously, and how long it changed for:

Do you have any ideas as to why your behaviour changed back?

Have you ever had a lasting change in belief?

If so, what made it so lasting?

Warming Up

Another area that is always a bone of contention is exercising before proceeding with any manual handling. It is difficult for many people to imagine themselves doing exercises before lifting a box or pushing a stock cage, however, it is important that you understand exercising. I have never been one of these trainers or consultants who tells people that they must jog on the spot for a minute, jump up and down or do the pelvic tilt a few times (although they have their place). In some workplaces I find that the majority of handling activities require more stretching of legs or shoulders etc… as in high manual handling jobs, walking and light lifting are excellent ways to warm the muscles up-making them supple and able to the perform the task.

When it comes to people warming up, be sensible in your approach-remember that exercising increases flexibility and strength. You are unlikely to see a sports person doing their physically demanding activity without warming up, therefore an employee who is warmed up and capable of a task is less likely to be injured during their physically demanding activity.

List here a few stretching/warm up exercises you could do before a manual-handling task:

Once an employee has learned good lifting and handling techniques and has information and support on maintaining a healthy back, the manual handling activities become easier. At this point, the business leaders can concentrate on how jobs are performed as workers go about their everyday activities. Making good manual handling techniques part of the job requirement is one of the keys to good manual handling performance.

Knowing how to recognise potential problems in manual handling activities and solving them is also part of the key to success.

Learning to evaluate tasks and identify risk areas is of importance. Consider the following:

1. Workstations that are too high or too low and require prolonged forward or backward bending
2. Heavy and awkward loads
3. Loads with sharp edges or risk of contamination
4. The environment such as: lighting (too dark, too bright), temperature, flooring
5. Repetitive twisting or bending
6. Frequent repetitive movements of the arms, hands or shoulders
7. Tasks requiring a great deal of sitting or standing in one position for prolonged periods of time
8. Will the manual handling involve reaching and stretching?
9. Tasks requiring a great deal of manual handling
10. Tasks performed in confined spaces
11. Tasks requiring good strength, flexibility and endurance
12. Tasks requiring prolonged intense concentration
13. Is the person physically capable?
14. Does the handling activity require special skills or knowledge?

27

Controlling Back Injuries

So far we have discussed the causes of back injuries and general methods of back injury prevention. In order to successfully reduce and, hopefully, prevent injuries from affecting the performance of employees, more detailed information is needed. Specifically, we need to learn more about:

1.   Worksite design and evaluation
2.   Good manual handling techniques
3.   Management of manual handling
4.   Manual handling risk assessment
5.   Communicating with employees
6.   Insurance and compensation
7.   Manual handling and the law

Understanding each of these points will help reduce back injuries in the workplace.

1.5 - Workplace Design and Assessment

Although we will look in more detail at risk assessments later in this handbook, there is much that everyone can do to make their workplace manual handling activities safer. Firstly; discussing an issue with others to establish whether they are having the same problem, see if they have been able to overcome it.

Case Study:

More and more I find that clients and their employees look externally for answers, not so long ago a client whose primary role was warehouse order picking, was having difficulty with injuries caused by falling stock (due to pyramid picking) this is where pickers take the nearest item causing half of the items above to be unsupported, then what happens another picker then takes the item on top of it, in essence removing the anchor and items then generally fall onto that picker causing injury (this is a common problem in warehousing) and the solution was a simple one, they introduced a near miss reporting programme, supported by a short introduction session at the beginning of shifts, and made it part of everyone's responsibility to highlight to each other problems and report them as needed. Meaning that; **nobody should turn a blind eye**. Initially people always feel a little apprehensive, but over a few weeks people start to come on board and as near miss reporting goes up, incidents and injuries start to reduce, ask **yourself what would you prefer in your workplace, high near miss reporting or a high rate of incidents and injuries**

Evaluating the workplace is something that everyone working there can get involved in. The evaluation is usually performed for new activities, or existing activities that have not previously been evaluated or have changed in some way. I have found, over the years, that doing an evaluation gives me far more insight about the workplace, the activities undertaken and, more importantly, the individuals carrying out these tasks. The purpose of evaluating our workplaces is to identify the full process; start – middle – end, within this, everyone can identify issues or causes of injury. When potential issues are identified, the workplace may be redesigned or modified to prevent, or seriously reduce, the risk of injuries occurring. Even if major workplace redesign is impractical, often simple and inexpensive modifications can be made to greatly reduce the risk.

Remember; one of the most important factors in workplace safety is people. Creating the right culture means that people are more likely to find solutions or to discuss concerns and help to resolve issues. Poor workplace cultures are more prone to individuals carrying on with practices that can lead to injury, because they feel that it is not their problem.

Case Study:

> A simple solution for a client was the use of manual
> handling gloves, these worked so well that within a year
> they had gone from a one size fits all grip glove to a
> specific fit grip glove that increased the persons grip by
> over five times.

Case Study:

> Another client who had to lift rolls weighing over 10kg of
> plastic wrap into a machine, found that simply by using
> the frame of the machine they only had to place it and
> slide it into position – In the past this client had built a
> platform for over the area so that they could be lowered
> into place below foot level.

Sometimes we over complicate the situation. I have found that the best manual handling advisors are those that do not mind discussing the issue with others. I myself have off days and occasionally we are so engrossed in the situation that we need to take that step back and chat with others to find the most suitable solution. I say most suitable, because you cannot please everyone all the time. This may be due to differences in the individuals involved in the task, there may be operational requirements, and another consideration is, dare I say, the dreaded cost. Yes you read correctly, cost is an important factor and as businesses exist to make money then it is a real issue that often has be overcome.

When I conduct these evaluations of workplaces, I also try to get involved in the activity. This helps in a number of ways; it allows me to work with the people doing the task, it allows me to truly understand the activity and it gives me some (generally not a great amount) creditably, it gives me the time to engage these individuals and in many cases prise out of them their real concerns. For larger operations involving lots of manual handling, these evaluations are invaluable for designing and modifying workplace activities.

If you are pulling your face at the statement above, go out and try one.

Another benefit of evaluating a workplace is targeting difficult or repetitive movements, which cannot be avoided. If the workplace cannot be modified, workers can be taught specific techniques which counteract difficult handling activities or positions.

1.6 - Ergonomics and Handling

To prepare for a workplace evaluation, the manager or supervisor must understand the basics of task design and modification.

There are a number of principles:

Firstly, managers, supervisors and employees alike should attempt to minimise the weight and bulk of a load. This will reduce the amount of pressure on the discs and joints we mentioned earlier by decreasing the force required and allowing objects to be kept close to the body when lifted.

Secondly, minimise the distance an object must be moved. The ideal height an object should be stored is waist height. This height removes the need for bending or leaning forward, and ultimately reduces the strain on the lower back. Reducing the distance that employees need to carry heavy loads to a minimum could mean using a trolley, cage or hand-operated truck.

The third principle is that of providing sufficient time for physically challenging tasks and allowing recovery time between these demanding or repetitive activities by spacing them throughout the day. This will reduce the overall amount of fatigue during a given period of time.

The fourth principle is cross training and rotation of workers through different activities as this is an effective way of distributing the workload, ensuring that no one individual has to work at a particularly physically demanding task for a long period of time.

List here what you believe could cause you back pain in your workplace (and remember to keep it simple):

What can you do about reducing the likelihood of suffering back pain?

Performing a Workplace Assessment

This next section of the book, although not specifically on manual handling, creates a good base for some of the principles we are to look at later. Remember what was stated earlier in this book, that posture and awkward tasks could also cause the back pain that people associate with manual handling.

A manager or supervisor should understand some basic design principles before completing a workplace assessment/evaluation. When they have the principles firmly in mind, they should begin evaluating the workplace by reviewing an activity or task; one that is believed to be more physically demanding than others. All the tasks in the workplace should then be carefully evaluated. The manager or supervisor should examine the positions their employees assume as they work.

Back pain can result from many different sources. Consider more than just the heavy lifting jobs. Potential problem areas include the following:

Workstations that are too low and require prolonged forward bending.

If the workstation is too low, an employee will be forced to stand or sit with the head and neck learning forward, shoulders slightly rounded and the lower back in a forward bent position (this posture increases strain on the a number of areas of the back and, most importantly, in the lower back, which can lead to pain). Prolonged forward bending is one of the most physically demanding activities for the back. In this position the spine including ligaments, tendons and the muscles are all under great tension, and a considerable force is placed on the discs, again this can lead to herniated discs as we have seen earlier in this book.

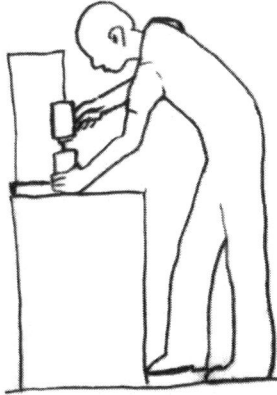

The aim is to try and find ways to reduce the need to bend forward. Can the workstation be raised? Ideally, the workstation should be adjustable. If the workstation is not adjustable, the fixed work height should be set at approximately 36 inches. This may be accomplished by simply placing raised supports under the legs of a workstation. The 36-inch work height allows the average employee to stand up straight, with the normal curve in the lower back and the head and shoulders erect. Shorter individuals or workers who must handle taller objects should stand on a platform or stool. If a low work position is unavoidable, the employee should be educated by the importance of alternating positions frequently and performing brief backward bending stretches throughout the day.

Work environments that are high and require prolonged backward bending.

Continuous working at or above shoulder level can be very physically demanding. This type of work requires hyperextension of the neck and back, causing increased pressure on the neck joints and an unequal distribution of forces on the spine as a whole. This type of activity repeated several times a day can lead to a number of painful upper back and shoulder problems. If an employee is required to reach overhead frequently or perform tasks which cause the elbows to exceed a 40 to 45 degree angle away from the sides or front of the body, management should attempt to either lower the work height or raise the worker. This can often be accomplished by using raised work platforms, rearranging storage areas or by providing stair platform ladders.
If an employee must spend a great deal of time reaching overhead in the backward bent position, he should be encouraged to change positions often and to perform brief forward bending stretches to relieve the joint stress and muscle fatigue.

Work that is too far away.

Regardless of whether the worker is standing or sitting, repetitive forward reaching at arm's length puts a great deal of pressure on the lumbar region of the back. When lifting in this way, the arms become levers and the back is the fulcrum. The longer the lever arm, the greater the pressure placed on the neck, arms and back. Reaching also causes an increased risk of injury to these structures even if heavy lifting is not being performed.

All manual handling activities should be performed in a way which allows efficient use of the arms and shoulders, without creating a long lever arm that transfers excessive force to neck, arms and lower back. This can often be accomplished by simply reinforcing the need for good manual handling techniques. When working at a table or workstation, employees should move their work as close to the edge as possible and position themselves close to the table. Workers should be taught to lift and carry loads close to their bodies.

When placing items on shelves, employees should be encouraged to set the item on the front edge and then slide it into position. When retrieving the object, they should follow the opposite procedure. The greatest amount of strength is available when working between shoulder and waist level, with the elbows tucked into the sides (ideally at a 90 degree angle)

Work activities that are performed in confined places or tasks that require repeated twisting.

If there is limited space for employees to manoeuvre and move objects, they will often twist the spine to accomplish the task. Repetitive twisting is one of the most damaging movements for the back. When twisting and bending movements are combined, the stress on the discs and facet joints can be extreme. Even though discomfort is not necessarily experienced at the time, damage may be occurring. Try to provide enough floor space so that the employee can pivot the feet when lifting or moving an item. No time is lost when the worker pivots instead of twists, and the stress is reduced dramatically. In some cases it helps to rearrange the work area so the lift is performed side-to-side rather than front to back. It may also help to place some items far enough apart that the employee must turn and step, rather than twist. Swivel chairs are helpful for workers who are sitting. The use of conveyors, chutes, slides and turntables can be used to change the direction of material flow.

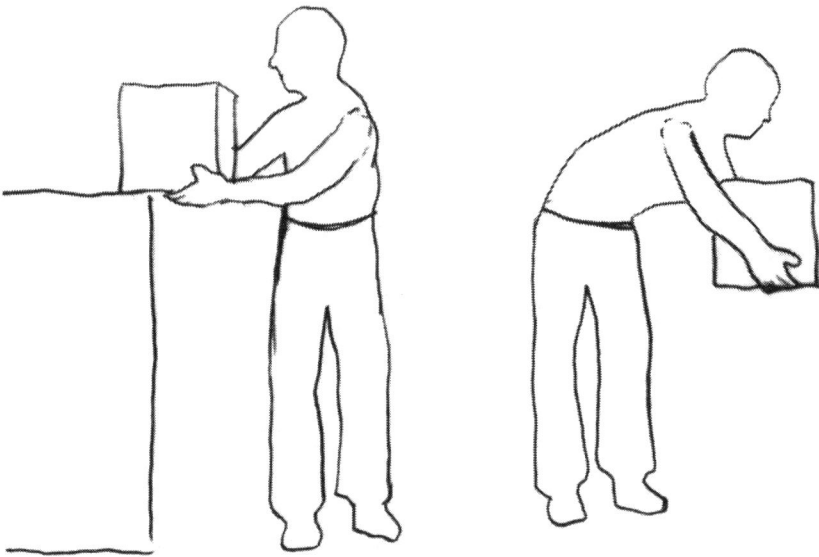

Tasks that require prolonged standing on hard concrete surfaces.

The muscles of the low back play a significant role in helping to maintain the standing position. Without occasional relief these muscles become fatigued. When this happens one begins to adopt a more slouched or forward bent posture and additional stress is placed on the lower back. There are a number of ways in which fatigue can be reduced. A foot rail, box or stool, which allows the worker to slightly elevate one-foot can also reduces stress. Rearranging the work so workers can alternate between standing and sitting tasks or allowing a brief stretching break periodically throughout the day may also be effective in reducing fatigue. I have also seen good results from rubber floor mats and cushioned shoe inserts as they also reduce the strain on the legs and the back.

Workstations that require sitting or standing in a static position for prolonged periods of time.

When work requires intense concentration or does not allow movement, the back can become tense because of fatigue or tiredness. It is important that some movement is provided to relieve the tension that occurs. Tasks that provide variation between sitting and standing activities cause decreased tension by providing normal joint and muscle movement.

Tasks that require prolonged sitting, particularly with the back unsupported.

Sitting is very stressful to the back especially if the employee slouches forward to complete the work activities. A high stool with no back or foot support is a common example of a workstation, which encourages the employee to assume a slouched position. In this position there is a great amount of pressure on the discs and the muscles. Tendons and muscles are stretched and weakened making the employee more prone to back injuries during manual handling activities. Sitting jobs should be designed so that 90-degree angles can be maintained at the elbows, hips and knees. Chairs and stools should provide support for the lower back and allow the feet to comfortably rest on the floor or a foot support. Stools should have footrests and chairs should be as adjustable as possible.

It is important again that everyone from managers to employees should be encouraged to get up and walk around periodically. Changing stressful positions frequently is the key.

Tasks that require frequent manual material handling.

This may not be a problem if good manual handling techniques are used. Anytime employees lift and carry objects there is potential for a problem. Manual tasks should be eliminated where practical and reduced through the use of lift tables, lift trucks, hoists, work dispensers, conveyors and similar mechanical aids when possible. Materials can be delivered to the worker by roller, caster tables, automatic conveyor systems or other means to totally eliminate the lifting and reaching tasks. One should follow the three principles of task design discussed earlier in this section.

Tasks that are awkward and oversized loads that are moved.

Manual handling of an awkward or oversized load can be difficult and dangerous if people do not stop to think about the situation and problem solve it. Employees should be encouraged to assess these loads and ask for help or use a lifting/moving device if they are unsure of their ability to handle the load safely.

If a load is oversized and is being handled manually, repackaging the material, using mechanical assistance or performing a team lift should be considered. If this is not practical, it is critical that instruction and information in good manual handling techniques be emphasised and reinforced on a regular basis through newsletters, changing posters, in team briefings etc... The key to lifting and carrying objects correctly is to maintain the normal curves in your spine throughout the movement. This involves keeping the head up, the stomach muscles tight (suck in that belly!), and the lower back arched. By bending the legs and keeping the lower back in normal alignment (not a vertically straight back), the movement will be taking place at the hips rather than at the waist. It is this movement at the hips that allows the person's legs to do the work, not the back.

Notes:

Notes:

Notes:

40

Part 2

Techniques and Practices

Part 2 – Techniques and Practices

2.1 - Manual Handling Techniques

In my opinion repeated poor manual handling is the major cause of back injuries. It is important that managers, supervisors and employees recognise the movements and activities that are the most physically demanding. Some of the common mistakes include:

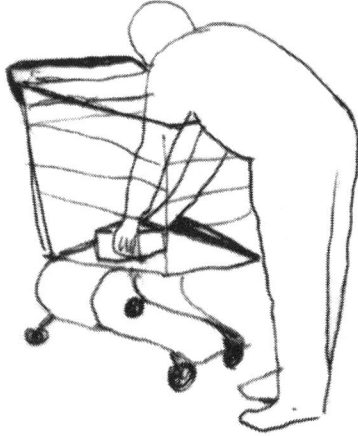

List here some of the common mistakes you feel you and others make when manual handling.

Now list here what you think are some of the good techniques you use should be:

Common Mistakes

Lifting with the back bent forward and the legs straight.
This places great amounts of pressure on the discs between the vertebra, the surrounding muscles, tendons and ligaments of the lower back.

Using fast jerking lifting motions.
Lifting objects that are difficult to grip, working in an area which is slippery or has tripping hazards, or trying to work too fast can prevent smooth safe lifting techniques.

Bending and twisting at the same time.
The motion of lifting creates enormous pressure in the lower back, and treats the lumbar region of the back like a cloth being wrung by twisting and flexing it. This movement causes some of the greatest wear and tear to the discs in your back.

Handling the load too far away.
Not bringing the load close to the body can cause significant injury. The stress increases five to ten times when a load is at arms length. For example, a one-kilogram weight at arms length away from the body will apply the same physical stress in the lumbar region of the back as holding a ten-kilogram weight close to the waist.

Poor preparation and planning.
Failing to pre-plan or test the load, checking the path of travel, or clearing an area for the object to be placed often leads to additional strain on the back.

Poor communication.
When two people are lifting together the movement must be coordinated. Any misunderstanding of instructions can also result in unnecessary risk.

Insufficient strength.
Many times a handling device is required to move objects safely. Lack of necessary equipment often results in unsafe lifting practices. When lifting devices are made available, employees should be trained *and be required* to use them when necessary. Injuries sometimes occur when handling devices are available but not used.

Managers and supervisors should survey the workplace and the use of good manual handling techniques should be reviewed. Employees should be required to follow the rules of good manual handling. Human nature means that we will all try to take lifting "shortcuts" which may appear to be easier or save time, and often individuals who have not experienced back pain do not think manual handling rules apply to them. Managers and supervisors must set and enforce the standards for safe lifting. All employees should review a "mental checklist". The rules of good manual handling include the following:

Rules of Good Manual Handling

Test the load.
> Prior to lifting or moving an object, test the weight of the load to make sure it can be moved safely. Use a lifting/handling device if necessary.

Plan the move.
> Check the path of travel/destination of the load to make sure it is clear. Clear the path before picking up the load.

Use a wide, balanced stance with one foot ahead of the other.
> A solid base of support reduces the likelihood of slipping and jerking movements.

Keep the lower back in its normal arched position while lifting.
> Bend at the knees or hips. With the back arched, the forces are more evenly distributed on the support structures.

Bring the load as close to the body as possible.
> This keeps your back from acting as a fulcrum and reduces the strain.

Keep the head and shoulders up as the lifting motion begins
> This helps to keep the arch in the lower back.

Tighten the stomach muscles as the lift begins.
> This causes the abdominal cavity to become a weight bearing structure, thus unloading the spine.

Lift with the legs and stand up in a smooth, even motion.
> Using the strength of the legs to straighten the knees and hips as the lift is completed decreases the lower back strain.

Move the feet (pivot) if a direction change is necessary.
> This eliminates the need to twist at the waist, thus significantly reducing the strain on the discs, muscles, tendons and ligaments of the back.

Communicate if two or more individuals are involved in the movement.
> This reduces the likelihood of an error that could result in sudden or jerking movements.

By following these simple rules, the physical strain on the discs, joints, muscles and ligaments are reduced. In this way, the cumulative factors that add up over time to produce a back problem are minimised.

Principles of Good Lifting:

This is the most common method for lifting and allows for full use of good manual handling techniques. To perform the diagonal lift the employee should establish a wide base of support and straddle the object with one foot slightly ahead of the other (on a diagonal). As the body is lowered, bending at the knees and hips, the worker should firmly grasp the far outer corner of the object with the hand that is on the side of the forward foot and then grasp the opposite side with the other hand.

Establishing a good grip is especially important because if the item slipped while lifting, the jerking movement could severely damage the low back structures (due to the performance I have seen from manual handling gloves I now always recommend them for most manual handling activities). The object should then be moved as close to the body as possible. Keeping the head and shoulders up while maintaining the normal arch in the lower back, the individual should straighten the knees and hips as he comes to a standing position. In a proper lift, the head will rise first with no movement in the back. In an improper lift, the hips will rise first requiring the back to bend forward while the lift is performed. The key to this technique is keeping the back arched and using the strength of the legs to lift.

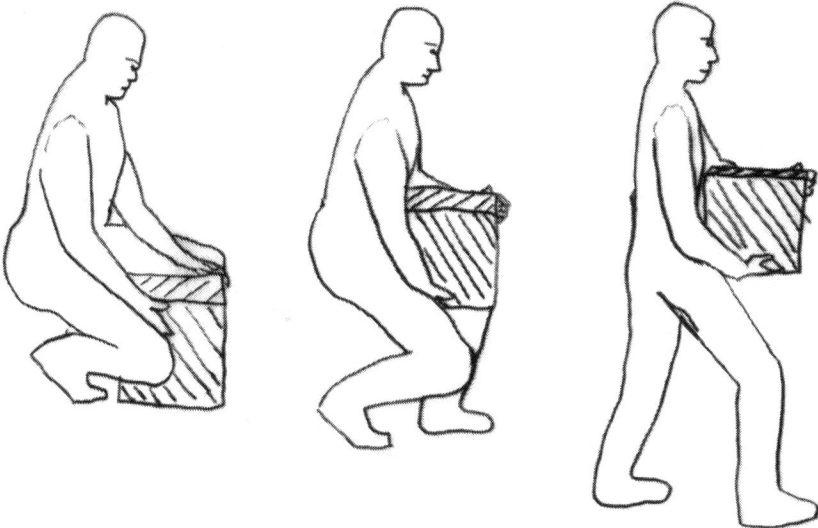

2.2 - Advanced Manual Handling Techniques

As mentioned above, the most common lifting techniques is the diagonal lift, however, we all live in the real world (well most of the time!), many of us place items in the boot of the car, or on shelves that require the use of steps. Due to the awkwardness of these situations, the next pages are dedicated to a number of lifting techniques that I have trained people in.

Lifting is one of the most physically demanding work activities, especially if the correct techniques are not used. As discussed in the previous section, there are a number of steps in performing a safe lift. Additionally, there are a number of techniques which can be used when lifting. The weight and size of the object, location or distance of the move, strength and flexibility of the individual, as well as other factors will dictate the method of lift deemed to be most appropriate. Over the following pages, differing techniques for lifting are discussed. Managers and supervisors should practice these methods with employees to ensure they can perform each technique. Some employees may not be able to complete each movement due to lack of strength or flexibility. If this is the case, the manager or supervisor should encourage modification of the lift to utilise the best manual handling techniques for each individual.

There are a number of techniques, which can be performed safely and will cover most lifting tasks.

Power Lift

The power lift allows the lifting of bulky or heavier loads with minimal strain (this technique is similar to that used by weightlifters). The individual should establish a wide, solid base with one foot positioned in front of the other. The body should be slightly over the load with the knees bent in a half squatting position. While bending at the hips, the object should be grasped firmly (recommend the use of grip gloves). No bending at the waist should take place. With the head and shoulders up, the hips and knees are then straightened to complete the lift.

At the beginning of the lift, it is important that the first movement is with the head, followed by the straightening of the legs. Once the item begins to move it can be pulled close to the waist as the hips straighten out.

Tripod Lift

This technique allows an individual to conveniently bring the item close to the body before completing the lift. The worker should place one foot beside the front portion of the object, and drop slowly to the other knee. Gripping the object firmly at both near and far corners with the head and shoulders up and the lower back arched, they should then lift or roll the object onto the top of the thigh. Maintaining the same posture, the worker can then stand with the object cradled. For many this will be the end of the lift but for those who are carrying over a longer distance the item can be placed on to a shoulder and balanced but only if the person is physically able to do so.

This lift should be avoided by employees with knee or shoulder problems but should be encouraged for those who do not have good arm strength.

Squat Lift:

This lifting technique is similar to the diagonal lift except that instead of straddling the object the employee squats in front of it with the feet and knees approximately shoulder width apart. This lift should only be used when lifting small light items or when insufficient space is provided to straddle the object.

The individual should lower into a full squat with knees bent and the lower back arched. The item should then be lifted with the arms and cradled close to the body. With the head and shoulders up, the legs should be used to lift. For added balance and assistance the employee should be encouraged to hold the object in one arm if possible, and complete the lift with the free hand on a fixed object such as a chair or counter. Individuals with knee problems should avoid this lift.

Partial Squat Lift (With And Without Support):

This lifting, or stooping, technique reduces the strain on both the back and the knees. For both techniques the feet should be positioned shoulder width apart with one foot slightly in front of the other if possible. For the partial squat with support, one hand should be placed on the forward thigh or a fixed object as the knees and hips are bent and the individual lowers themselves to pick the item up.

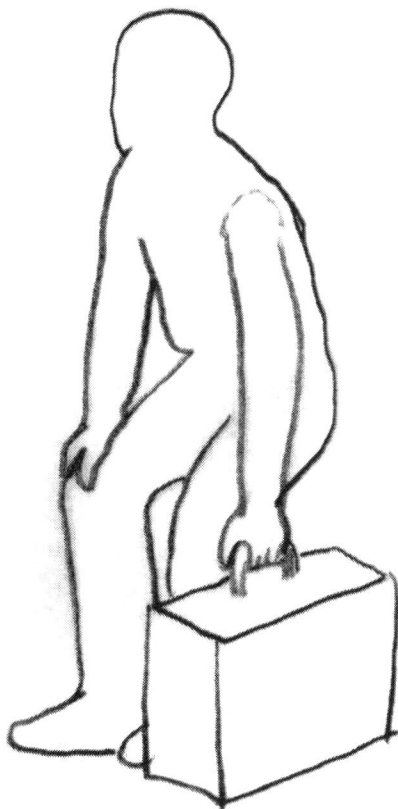

Keeping the lower back arched and the head and shoulders up, pull the object close, complete the lift and push off with the supporting hand as the individual stands up. The partial squat lift without support is helpful for lifting heavy or bulky items, which are placed on a surface near knee height. Bending at the knees and hips helps to avoid forward bending at the waist.

Golfer's Lift:

This lifting technique is often used by individuals who have knee problems, have decreased leg strength or must lift where there is a barrier in front of the item: like a boxed crate. For this technique, place one hand on a fixed object to support the upper body. The individual should arch the back, bend at the hips and raise one leg behind him. By raising the leg, the upper body weight is counterbalanced and bending of the lower back is reduced. To pick up the item the individual should look up, push off with the free hand and lower the raised leg.

Straight Leg Lift:

The straight leg lift technique is used when the knees and hips cannot be bent. There are times when items must be lifted over immoveable obstructions, from containers, or from the boot of a car. In these situations one of the more practical and safer methods is the straight leg lift.

Special care must be taken to minimise the potential for strain when individuals perform this technique. To begin, the individual should position themselves as close to the object as possible with the knees slightly bent. If the individual is reaching over something like the lip of a boot on a car, they should press their legs forward against the fixed object over which they are reaching. While bending slowly at the hips, not the waist the individual should firmly grasp the item and bring it closer if necessary. With the lower back arched and the head up rotating the hips backward into a full standing position completes the lift.

When performing this lifting technique correctly, the muscles in the back of the legs will pull back on the hips and control the lifting movement. Individuals who have hamstring muscle injuries or lack of hip mobility will have difficulty with this technique.

Overhead Lift:

Extreme care should be used when moving objects overhead. Due to the arms being lifted, it is difficult to maintain balance and the potential for lower back and shoulder strain increases. To lift an object overhead, the individual should hold it close to the body and establish a comfortable stance with one foot ahead of the other and shoulder width apart. The individual should use the arm and shoulder muscles to raise the load whilst balancing their weight between the front and back feet. This will keep the load close to the centre of gravity and allow the individual to keep the normal arch in the lower back. As the weight is lifted overhead and toward the shelf, the individual should shift their weight forward onto the front foot, keeping the stomach muscles pulled in and the lower back immobile. Once in contact with the shelf, the weight should be pushed into place. The pushing motion removes the physical strain from the muscles and joints. To remove an item from overhead, the procedure should be reversed and weight should be shifted onto the back foot as the load is lowered. This technique will feel awkward unless the item is held very close to the worker's body. It should feel as though the item is either sliding up or down the chest and abdomen.

Pushing and Pulling Techniques

When pushing and pulling items, people often make the mistake of jerking with the whole of their body weight, unusually pivoting on their heels. The mistake here is that the body is unbalanced and creates a great amount of strain across the shoulders and upper back. As a first aider, I have even had to treat people for strains to the wrists and hernias due to this type of physical handling.

To help understand the best dynamics for pushing and pulling I have included some information on hand pump trucks and roll cages

When using such equipment, it is important that you make sure it is in a good state of repair- the last thing anyone needs when pulling a pallet, is one of the wheels not turning or to stop moving as you are manoeuvring it.

Over the years I have come across many so called best practices and beliefs regarding moving hand pump trucks and roll cages, however I have found the most useful to be the following technique:

Stand in such a manner that when gripping the device your arms have some flex at the elbow, then place your feet shoulder width apart, one foot slightly forward, again with flex in the knees. Then push forward or pull backwards by using the muscles in the legs. This reduces strain across the shoulders and both the upper and lower back. The other advantage of this technique is that you will be unable to move items that are simply too heavy for one person to move, or those which place individuals at increased risk of injury

Using these techniques ensures the individual is able to counteract or stop the motion. To do this, simply grip the device head on, keeping flex in the elbows and create a solid stance (feet shoulder width apart one foot slightly forward) with the knees unlocked and again use the leg muscles to push against the motion.

When training people in these techniques individuals have been amazed at how effective it is to get loaded devices moving and then stop them safely and securely.

Loading and Unloading Vans and Estate Cars

Loading of transit style vans and estate cars has been of concern to many of the clients I have worked with over the years. With this in mind I have decided to put some simple information in this guide

Loading a vehicle to many seems difficult due to headroom and the need to step in and out of vans, however, through many activities, I have found that the best way for any loading of vans is by simply placing items on the edge of a van floor and sliding them into place.

Some time ago I had the opportunity to work with one of my client's delivery drivers. This particular driver was prone to a good deal of time off each year with back pain, he linked this directly to loading and unloading of the van. After working with this driver doing one of my workplace evaluations, I found two problem areas; the first was the set up of the van's seat, the other problem was that he had only ever been taught to lift a box cube in a classroom (not once had he ever had any training or advice on the job). By the end of his shift he was uncomfortable, and he described his discomfort as a dull ache. I explained what my observations had highlighted and why I believed he was suffering. I advised and coached him on some things he could do to reduce the issues for himself. At first he was not accepting any of it, health and safety rubbish was his basic answer.

Over the years I have come across this initial response many times, but my experience has taught me that people are always eager to prove you wrong and themselves right. So I gave him a challenge; to set the seat up correctly first thing every morning, and to lift the way I had been lifting and coaching him throughout the day. With the support of his line manager, I visited the driver twice more over the next month and on one visit was able to work a shift along side him. The visits were to check that he was in fact playing by the rules of our agreement.

To end the challenge I met with the driver and observed and asked questions about how he had approached different situations and about his health, he explained "by the end of my shift, I used to have a dull ache in my back and sometimes in my shoulders, yet now after taking up this challenge I feel great, don't get me wrong, I am still physically tired, but I am able to now socialise and feel able to take part in doing stuff about the house".

He explained to me several times that initially it was taking him longer on the deliveries and he was getting some flack from customers and his line manager, but now he believed that he takes no more time than he previously took, "except I am now lifting and moving in better ways, it was just about getting used to it".

I know a number of you are saying that if I were to do that with all our drivers it would either cost me a fortune or take up so much time that there would be no time for anything else in the job. These occurrences, however, are rare, over the years I have only needed to do a small number of these types of sessions, as many of these employees become champions of the cause, as did this particular driver. This driver is now one of the client's role model drivers, someone who inducts all new delivery drivers and retrains all existing drivers, so it is important to weigh up all factors before dismissing such an idea.

Delivery drivers and sales persons are some of the most at risk people when it comes to manual handling and posture pain, and simple techniques can be a real lifesaver.

Loading and unloading cars is a particular risk for manual handling, especially from the rear of the vehicle due to the lip that most vehicles have. Interestingly, my time spent with St. John Ambulance as a casualty and patient-handling trainer taught me the most effective way of storing items in the boot of a car, and allowing good manual handling to be adopted. It is a technique that many people I train in manual handling skills often sit back in amazement at the simplicity of it all. I simply use a drag sheet approach these days, and train others using the same approach, which is, to place a dust sheet on the base of the boot, load items just onto the inside of the vehicle's floor and slide items into place, then when removing items further back I simply pull the dust sheet and, like a miracle, the item moves forward to the point I and others can lift items safely. It is also possible to use this technique in vans.

Manual Handling Whilst Sitting

Manual handling whilst sitting is not only unnatural but it places considerable stress on the lumber region of the back as all the weight and moving happens in this area.

Generally a sitting person can only handle one-fifth of the weight i.e. can lift less when sitting than they can when standing.

I once had a person compare this activity to something most of us have done over the years, they said "Lee, it is interesting that you mention this, as only last night, I took the family to a drive thru restaurant, and as I leaned through the car window and took hold of 4 drinks on a tray, I felt my back tense up to the point that I had to go and rest when we got home, this morning I can still feel the effects and every time I lean forward I can feel the discomfort".

Manual handling whist sitting should be avoided where possible, however, in the cases where no other method presents itself, assess the activity and see what can be done to reduce the risk of injury.

Moving of Drums

Drums, kegs and barrels can be difficult to manoeuvre, however, there are simple techniques that can help individuals manually handle these loads in a safe and effective manner.

If moving cylindrical loads on your own, they should be rolled, making sure that you keep one hand on it at all times to keep control of its speed and direction. At the same time, make sure that you are flexing your knees and keeping your back in alignment.

Should a cylindrical load need moving whilst it is upright, then an assessment should be carried out and the use of a lifting/moving aid should be considered.

It is possible to move barrels whilst they are upright, with relative ease, depending up on the surface, making sure that, if pushing it, the force of pushing is as low down the load as possible. This helps stop the weight wanting to push down into the floor on the side furthest away.

Manual Handling on Steps

Lifting on steps has been considered by many people over the years as dangerous and should be done away with. I have, however, come across many organisations and businesses that, out of necessity, must manually handle items whilst using ladders and safety steps.

Working at height, in my opinion, should be assessed and controls put in place where it is likely for a person to injure themselves should they fall, excluding fixed stairs (in the UK refer to the Work at Height Regulations 2005).

Procedures should be put in place to help prevent someone becoming injured whilst manually handling an item on steps or safety steps.
My preferred method for training individuals to manually handle at height is to use safety steps. Safety steps have fixed treads, a working platform with a handrail and side handrails. They are usually mobile by the use of wheels and incorporate a mechanism for prevention of moving the wheels whilst in use. By design, the wheels cannot be on the floor with the steps in the usable upright position. A lever device is supplied to lock the wheels, this lever must be operated to lock the wheels before the steps are used, or the wheels may be spring-loaded and retract as the ladder is used due to the weight of the user.

Footstools are great devices for obtaining extra height, so that you can reach items above shoulder height.

Safety steps and small stepladders should be used for accessing items that would normally be above head height, therefore allowing you to take the items down without the possibility of pulling them onto your head.

When using stools or steps, you should always take the time to position them correctly and make sure that they are set up in the proper manner. Step up, or walk up, and down steadily where possible use your hand to hold the steps or handrail whilst moving as it will help you from becoming unbalanced.

When required to lift on these devices, it is important to create a solid stance and one method I have found that works very well is using the same technique as on a level surface. One foot should be slightly in front of the other with space between the feet I manage this by placing one foot on one step and the other one either below or above, depending which way I will be lifting. I then place my feet towards the outside of the steps, which means that I can manoeuvre safely, using my feet to position myself more squarely onto the step then lift the items that need moving.

I have also found that it is far easier to rest items on the step, whilst getting off and then picking them up off the steps once I am on the ground.

Team Lifting

List here what you think you might need to consider when lifting with others:

```
┌─────────────────────────────────────────────────────────────┐
│                                                               │
│                                                               │
│                                                               │
│                                                               │
└─────────────────────────────────────────────────────────────┘
```

List here what steps you think you need to take when lifting with others:

```
┌─────────────────────────────────────────────────────────────┐
│                                                               │
│                                                               │
│                                                               │
│                                                               │
└─────────────────────────────────────────────────────────────┘
```

Team lifting is one area of manual handling that often gets forgotten, but it is a key requirement for people to be trained and instructed in. Over the years I have trained many people from a great many industries in manual handling. I have not yet come a across a person who has never lifted with another.

Write down here what lifting with others you have done in the past:

```
┌─────────────────────────────────────────────────────────────┐
│                                                               │
│                                                               │
│                                                               │
└─────────────────────────────────────────────────────────────┘
```

Now think about what issues/problems you had (if any) and why they occurred:

```
┌─────────────────────────────────────────────────────────────┐
│                                                               │
│                                                               │
│                                                               │
│                                                               │
└─────────────────────────────────────────────────────────────┘
```

Communication is the key to team lifting, make sure that everyone understands what is going to happen, what they are expected to do, and where the item is going. This all sounds simple but I have seen many times (and I am sure many people reading this will have experienced it too) that you lift an item, and then you problem solve whilst carrying the item, which generally increases the chances of injury to you and the others you are lifting with.

Put a system in place like a count 123, lift etc... and use the same system for putting the item down. In my experience I have found that this is the largest single cause of manual handling injuries when two or more people are lifting items together. I have only one thing to say about team lifting **Communicate, Communicate, Communicate.**

2.3 - Additional Lifting Hints

It is important to remember that when lifting heavy or bulky items it may be necessary to use a lifting device or team lift. If this is not possible, the employee should be provided sufficient time to plan and complete any difficult lift. The diagonal and modified diagonal lifts are especially recommended for heavy or awkward loads.

Daily situations often require employees to lift items in a variety of positions. Making a lift totally risk-free is nearly impossible. The goal is to perform a particular lift in the "best way possible". If workers learn to review the brief "mental checklist" and incorporate as many of those components as possible into the lift they will be actively assuming responsibility for their own back care.

It is important that you test a load before lifting. By testing the weight you can also in most cases, decide if the load is likely to shift whilst being moved, i.e. liquids like water or oil etc..., even partially filled boxes can have their contents move whilst being carried. Due to the effects of the contents of a box moving whilst being carried, always test the item immediately before moving it.

The above brings me on to another area that I have a great deal of experience in, and that is moving people. My advice here is always: move and deal with the individual needing to be moved in a way that you would like to be treated. In essence, talk to the person - tell them what you are going to do, and talk them through it, be reassuring. If possible wrap the individual in something (like a blanket, a jacket) so that it is difficult for them to reach out and grab at stationary objects such as door frames. One of the most instinctive reflexes is to reach out when they feeling out of control, a tactic I have used to get around this particular difficulty is not only to wrap them in a blanket but to give them something to hold on to, for example; the strap of a carry chair or a handbag.

Notes:

62

Notes:

Notes:

Part 3

Managing and Supervising

Part 3 – Managing and Supervising

3.1 - Management of Manual Handling

Managing manual handling activities is key to good management. All too often people see manual handling and safety as an add on to their activities, but it is interesting that the same qualities of managing manual handling and heath and safety are the very same skills set for supervising, managing and leading others.

Risk Assessment

Risk assessment is not a new idea; we have all been doing risk assessments since we were taught how to cross the road. The principles of formal risk assessment and required action in the UK were set out in 1974 when the **Health and Safety at Work etc. Act 1974** was put into force. This is one of the first pieces of major health and safety legislation that removed the instruction to businesses, instead requiring each individual business to evaluate and take reasonable actions to take care of health and safety for both employees and anyone else who may be affected by the work activities of the business.

Since these early days, regulations have been created to support the Act of 1974. Particular to manual handling, the main two are:
The Management of Health and Safety at Work Regulations 1999 - placing a specific requirement for businesses to conduct risk assessments and apply appropriate controls.
The Manual Handling Operations Regulations 1992. Although these regulations have been revised and expanded beyond their original intention, they interestingly do not specify any particular method of carrying out risk assessments and, as a result there are many, many different systems in use.

Experience has shown me that risk assessments, particularly those for manual handling, do not have to be time consuming provided that the format used allows early recording and the process of evaluating any risk is simple.

A requirement of these regulations is that results of risk assessments must be suitable and sufficient and recorded in writing where there are five or more employees.

Risk assessment is a key tool for the successful management of health and safety and, in particular, manual handling activities.

When looking at risk assessment, we first must have a clear understanding of what is meant by the terms 'hazard' and 'risk'.

Write down here what you believe a hazard to be.

```
```

What is a risk?

```
```

The whole purpose of a manual handling risk assessment is for employers, managers and others in the workplace to work out what the problems are:

> **Hazards** – how much of a problem each one is;

> **Risks** –work out appropriate controls.

There are two types of risk assessment, which are not mutually exclusive. The first is a quantitative risk assessment, which is produced on a probability estimate; the other type is a qualitative risk assessment, which is more subjective, based on personal judgement backed by generalised data on risks. For the most part qualitative risk assessments are much simpler and are adequate for a large percentage of work activities.

What skills do you think make a person competent to carry out a manual handling risk assessment?

```
```

List here the main pieces of legislation we discussed earlier concerning manual handling:

```
```

Explain the duties an employer has regarding manual handling in the workplace:

```



```

What duties do employees have regarding manual handling in the workplace?

```



```

What do you think "so far as is reasonably practicable" means?

```



```

When starting a risk assessment for manual handling, start by walking around the workplace and look afresh at the manual handling activities and ask yourself what could reasonably be expected to cause harm. Ignore the trivial and concentrate on significant hazards, which could result in serious harm or effect several people.

Ask others (supervisors, employees etc…) what they think. They may have noticed things, which are not immediately obvious. Talking to others in the workplace helps to examine in detail the manual handling activities and will lead to decisions on what the risks of the activity are and how these can be avoided or reduced by the use of control measures.

As part of the manual handling assessment the following should be assessed:

- ❑ The task being carried out
- ❑ The load to be moved
- ❑ The environment that the manual handling activity will be taking place in
- ❑ Take a look at the capabilities of the individual or individuals involved in the manual handling operation

Before we take a closer look at the risk assessment process for manual handling let us first ask some questions:

What might be involved in a manual handling task?

What things might you need to consider about the load?

Are there any environmental issues which may affect the way you manually handle?

What might you need to consider about yourself and others involved in the manual handling activity?

Manual Handling Procedures

Once manual handling risk assessments have been carried out, the worst thing to do, in my opinion is place the assessment into a file that nobody ever reads; people only take things seriously when they are aware. Having a periodic refresher on manual handling issues ensures that everyone remains aware.

Over the years I have experienced many different methods of informing the general workforce of manual handling risk assessments.

During this time, I have found one that is the best all-round fit, and not just for manual handling, the design and use of a Manual Handling Procedure.

Giving the procedure a user friendly title, such as, 'Taking the pain out of Manual Handling' is a great way to create a lasting impact. A good way to set these procedures out is:

1. Sign up to Procedure Page
2. Purpose
3. Scope
4. Procedure
5. Documentation
6. Responsibility
7. Training
8. Audit & Reviewing
9. Glossary of terms
10. Appendixes

These procedures should be as short and to the point as possible, and reviewed as required or at a set time once a year, every three years for low risk activities etc…

It is important they are customised to your business, that they are written in the language that the life blood of your workplace understands and is able to put into practice. All too often I go to workplaces that have had a health and safety consultant visit and provide them with a great looking manual, and yet the individuals carrying out the task have in, most cases, not seen it. Of the few that have seen the manual none remember its contents as it is too full of section 1 blah blah blah, and regulation10 of… blah blah blah.

My advice to you in the pursuit of a health and safety manual is keep it simple. Create easy to read procedures and policies that basically explain what you want and what you do not want employees to do. Where the risks are high, explain to them why they must follow these procedures or policies. Get them to sign to it when you introduce the procedure, when you have a new starter, when you update a procedure, if the employee is involved in an incident relating to one of more of the procedures etc…
Procedures will help to create a good safety culture, they will allow people to see credible health and safety controls that keep them safe, without having to read through the 5000 risk assessments that many businesses seem to have.

Personal Protective Equipment

When it comes to personal protective equipment, manual handling grip gloves and safety shoes as a minimum.

Does grip affect the way you manual handling items?

```
┌─────────────────────────────────────────────────────┐
│                                                       │
│                                                       │
│                                                       │
│                                                       │
└─────────────────────────────────────────────────────┘
```

Have you ever dropped or nearly dropped an item due to grip? If so, what was it? What were the consequences?

```
┌─────────────────────────────────────────────────────┐
│                                                       │
│                                                       │
│                                                       │
│                                                       │
└─────────────────────────────────────────────────────┘
```

Could better grip have reduced or stopped it from happening?

```
┌─────────────────────────────────────────────────────┐
│                                                       │
│                                                       │
│                                                       │
│                                                       │
└─────────────────────────────────────────────────────┘
```

Other than grip, list here other advantages of wearing gloves whilst handling items:

```
┌─────────────────────────────────────────────────────┐
│                                                       │
│                                                       │
│                                                       │
│                                                       │
└─────────────────────────────────────────────────────┘
```

Let us for a short while investigate the use of gloves. Research shows that simply by wearing leather gloves can improve your grip 3 to 5 times that of the skin. With some specific manual handling grip gloves this could be as high as 10 to 15 times that of the skin.

Besides from providing extra grip, manual handling gloves also help to reduce the pressure on your hand and help to protect from cuts and scrapes.

Other Manual Handling Aids etc…

When trying to reduce the risk of injury through manual handling we always have to investigate the use of other controls. This may be by an ergonomic approach, leading to a reduction in manual handling risks and could lead to optimising the productivity of the task.

It is my experience that in many cases, productivity can be improved with some changes and costs, and most of the activities I have been involved in have been at a very low cost, some just a few man-hours of cost.

There are many mechanical handling aids about, this could be a simple lever that reduces the required force to move a load. Powered vacuum lifts are another very useful tool for lots of repetitive handling of medium and heavy weighted items. Hoists and mobile gantries are other effective mechanical aids that can help reduce the risks of manual handling.

With the world wide web at our fingertips finding solutions to handling problems should not be difficult, however, difficulty lies in deciding upon the right one. If in doubt get a second opinion, have an external consultant or advisors to provide help. On a number of occasions I have saved clients a fortune, just by being the fresh pair of eyes. As I have mentioned a number of times through this book. Keep it simple.

Accident Investigation

When accidents of any kind occur, managers and/or supervisors are usually required to conduct an accident investigation. The purpose of this is to find the cause of injury so control actions can be taken to prevent a future incident or accident occurring. All too often though, investigators have a difficult time pinpointing the exact cause. This is particularly true with back injuries or incidents involving manual handling operations.

Confusion and frustration is often the result. Investigations are looked on in different ways depending on who is conducting them. Insurance companies look for liability, trainers and consultants look for teaching material and case studies, and enforcement officials look for blame and failings. From the viewpoint of learning and prevention, it is important that you look at what led to the incident. Were there any warning signs before the incident occurred? Was the incident lessened by procedures that were in place? What training was given? Does this training need updating? and so on.

As I mentioned earlier, manual handling should have a procedure and I feel that incident reporting and investigation should too. This will lead to a

74

defined process for reporting all incidents, no matter how trivial they appear to be. During my employment as a manager for small and large businesses I found that a great many accidents were foreseeable and controllable long before they occurred. For the past eight years, I have found that the introduction of near miss reporting creates a great level of attention. A period of heightened awareness follows, which shows great impact on not only reduced numbers of incidents but generally a much improved working environment, pride in the workplace and the work that takes place, improving quality and productivity in many cases.

When back injuries are investigated, investigators often try to correlate the injury with a task that requires heavy lifting. Or the employee relates his injury to the work activity in which the pain was first noticed. Many times the cause listed in the accident report involves a relatively simple movement that does not necessarily involve lifting. The resulting question from the investigator and management is, "How could something so minor cause such a major injury?" The answer is easy. That particular task probably *did not* cause the injury.

As was discussed earlier in this book, back injuries are caused by the cumulative effect of five factors: poor posture, poor manual handling, physically demanding work, living habits, loss of body flexibility and poor physical fitness. These are very important factors that need to be remembered when conducting an accident investigation.

Below is the framework I use for investigating incidents and accidents:

Front page:

- ❑ Reference number
- ❑ Name of person involved in the incident
- ❑ Supervisor's name
- ❑ Address where accident took place
- ❑ Specific location incident took place
- ❑ Date and time of incident
- ❑ Date and time work ceased
- ❑ Was the individual absent from work for more than three days?
- ❑ Date individual returned to work
- ❑ Have alternative duties been considered and put in place, if so, what, when and how?
- ❑ Was the incident reported to the enforcing authorities?
- ❑ Was the individual seen by a medical doctor?
- ❑ Did the individual attend hospital, if so, which one?
- ❑ Date and time investigation started
- ❑ Date and time investigation was completed

The following headings are those I use as a basis for incident/accident investigations:

1. Reference number
2. Type of accident
3. Potential of injuries
4. Summary of investigation
5. Investigation committee
6. History leading to incident/accident
7. Relevant factors
8. Summary statement of cause leading to incident/accident
9. Root cause analysis
10. Action(s) recommended to prevent a reoccurrence
11. Line manager/supervisor comments
12. Leading investigator or health & safety officers comments

Any verbal information given should be written down and agreed as correct by the individual giving the information, always sign and date these statements.

I tend to ask people to provide me with a written statement and verbally question any points that I require further information on, I find that this helps me personally, or I have conducted investigations where I have taken detailed notes, any of these items here are personal choice. I like to understand and reflect on the environment where incidents have taken place, so I tend to take photos and have even on the odd occasion videotaped the activity.

Equipment I might use, (this list depends on the type, the potential and the result of the incident):

Report form, and checklist
Notepad and clipboard
Digital camera for instant pictures
Tape measure
Site plans
Meters (if needed) i.e. tape measures, noise metres, air monitors etc…
My own personal protective equipment.
    Safety shoes
    Hard hat
    Safety glasses
    Gloves

A key point to remember in all investigation is that the injured person and witnesses should be seen as soon as possible following the incident.

Root Cause Analysis

A root cause analysis should be a simple tool, over the years I have seen some very complicated modules, but I always use the following process

Why? Why? Why? Why? Why?

Root cause analysis is a great complimentary tool and, in my opinion, a necessity to any effective accident investigation. Deciding on the root cause is key to prevention, as too is highlighting contributory factors that led to the incident.

I personally start root cause analysis by listing the incident in the incident box i.e. Strain Back Muscle. Then I ask myself "Why did this happen?" Depending upon the situation, I may come up with answers like; the load was heavy, lack of equipment, lack of help, poor training, poor process in place. Once I have a list of initial findings, I ask "why?" to each of these findings. Again I list the findings in the next stage, and ask the question "why?" as many times as is needed to discover the root cause.

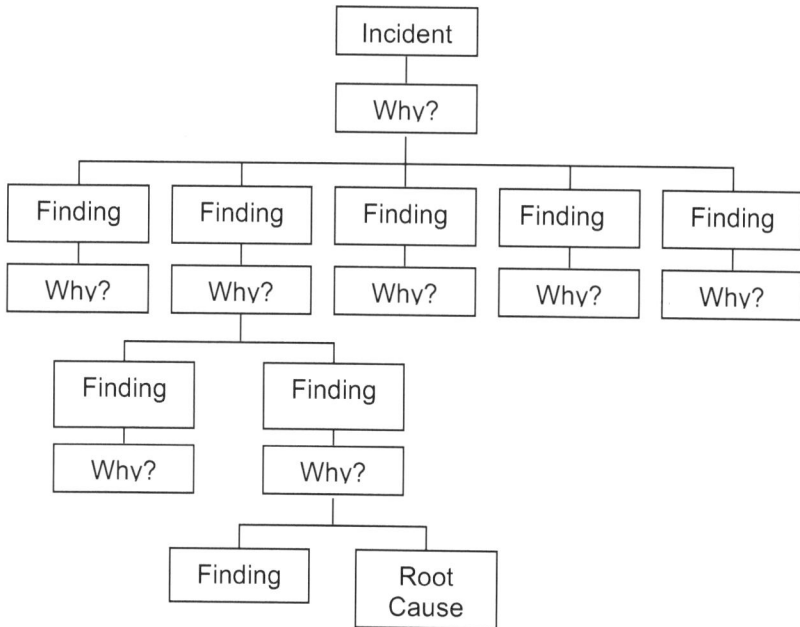

```
                        ┌──────────┐
                        │ Incident │
                        └──────────┘
                             │
                        ┌──────────┐
                        │   Why?   │
                        └──────────┘
                             │
  ┌─────────┬──────────┬─────┴────┬──────────┬──────────┐
┌───────┐ ┌───────┐ ┌───────┐ ┌───────┐ ┌───────┐
│Finding│ │Finding│ │Finding│ │Finding│ │Finding│
└───────┘ └───────┘ └───────┘ └───────┘ └───────┘
┌───────┐ ┌───────┐ ┌───────┐ ┌───────┐ ┌───────┐
│ Why?  │ │ Why?  │ │ Why?  │ │ Why?  │ │ Why?  │
└───────┘ └───────┘ └───────┘ └───────┘ └───────┘
              │
     ┌────────┴────────┐
 ┌───────┐       ┌───────┐
 │Finding│       │Finding│
 └───────┘       └───────┘
 ┌───────┐       ┌───────┐
 │ Why?  │       │ Why?  │
 └───────┘       └───────┘
                     │
            ┌────────┴────────┐
        ┌───────┐       ┌───────┐
        │Finding│       │ Root  │
        └───────┘       │ Cause │
                        └───────┘
```

Etc...

Once you master this type of root cause analysis, there are few things you will be unable to analyse.

78

Communicating with Employees

Offering meaningful feedback to employees on a regular basis is one of the most effective means of back injury prevention. Providing positive feedback about good manual handling techniques and lifting methods will always be more effective than criticising techniques. There are several methods of providing feedback including:

- ❑ Encouraging employees to use good manual handling techniques or handling aids when appropriate.
- ❑ Approaching an employee who is manually handling in an unsafe manner and expressing concern for his welfare, rather than condemnation. Tone of voice and choice of words can make a big difference in whether or not the employee will make an active effort to prevent injury or not.
- ❑ Making safe manual handling techniques a company policy. If the use of good manual handling is company policy, there will be no misunderstanding as to why managers and supervisors are concerned.
- ❑ Discussing with the employees any difficulties they may be having in implementing the use of good manual handling techniques. It is important that they feel they are able to take part in the process of protecting themselves from injury, and their suggestions will be considered.

Lets look at how we communicate, how do you listen when someone is talking to you?

What facial expressions would you like to see whilst taking to another employee?

79

What can body language tell you?

```



```

If you have a safety newsletter, include manual handling information and back injury data, either from your own business or the national accident rates of manual handling incidents.

There are many free newsletters out there; one is the Real World – Risk, Safety, Training & Projects newsletter free from the web www.realworld-rstp.com
Many clients have been getting these particular newsletters from the website and printing enough copies for canteen tables, breakout areas, etc.

Observing individual behaviour patterns can help identify potential problems, and can provide clues when something is wrong.

Behaviours that may indicate potential problems include:

1.   Personal adaptations made to worksites
2.   Changes in productivity rates
3.   Facial expressions (grimacing, pained expressions)
4.   Holding a particular body part (placing a hand on the lower back or rubbing a shoulder)
5.   Increased complaints about work
6.   Increased absenteeism
7.   Frequent changing of posture

It is important to develop a system where the employees can offer recommendations for possible workplace changes. Since they are performing the activities on a regular basis, your employees are often the best source for ideas and solutions. They may not be able to give you specific ideas for ergonomic changes, but will be able to give you valuable insight into where the difficulties are, and what potential issues may arise from a new process.

Also, if new changes are about to be implemented, then have a number of employees to act as champions for good lifting and the new process etc… this is a great way to develop change and maximise the effects of development.

By being able to recognise activities that place an employee at risk, the problems can be addressed before an injury actually occurs. This saves the company money and the employees are spared the pain and suffering of a back injury.

Employees need to know their concerns are heard. Managers and supervisors need to recognise those, often unspoken, parts of communication.

3.2 - Managing Back Injuries

It is unfortunate that even with a total commitment to prevention, with all employees playing their part, with good manual handling practices some back injuries will still occur. When they do, the reaction of managers and supervisors and their follow-up behaviour will have a major impact on the overall development and seriousness of that injury.

Back injuries are costly to everyone, not just companies. These costs, regardless of whether the injury occurs at work or at home, are usually paid entirely by the employer, both through insurance premiums and through higher overheads, through loss of production or costs for temporary staff etc.... The result is usually a lower level of profitability or a higher consumer price for your businesses products or services. The injured employee pays a different price, measured not only by the pain and suffering, but also through loss of wages and earning potential.

Insurance and Compensation

Since the focus of this handbook is "on-the-job" back injuries, it is necessary to discuss briefly how the liability insurance works.

Employers are required by law to provide employees with liability insurance; this is protection against injuries and illnesses that are work related. This insurance may be purchased from insurance companies or self-funded. Due to the complexity of the various types of coverage and differences in laws between not only UK countries but also European and internationally, it is difficult to discuss all aspects of employer liability insurance. In the UK claimants must establish a breach tort of negligence. A claim is usually made up of a payment for pain and suffering, payment of medical expenses and payment of any lost earnings (this is what most employees are more concerned about). If lost work time occurs or if there is a resulting disability, payments are made to the employee for these losses as well. The purpose of employer liability insurance is two fold: First, to compensate an injured employee in a fair manner, and second, to limit the liability exposure of the employer.

Sometimes managers and supervisors have a negative opinion of how the insurance compensation works. All too often, claims drag on and the costs seem to escalate. It does not have to be this way. Back injury claims can be controlled although many present insurance professionals are changing their view due to the claim culture we live in.

Claims Control and Management

A vital part of any business management activity is controlling compensation claims. Traditionally, the insurance company has processed claims. The insurance company and the medical professionals who are involved have been allowed to "handle" the claim until they are satisfied that the case has reached a conclusion. Keeping the total cost of the claim as low as possible has not necessarily been a priority.

In order to control the costs of medical disability benefits, and to return injured employees to work as soon as possible, managers and supervisors must become actively involved in every claim.

It must be understood that claims control does not in any way diminish the need for active incident/accident and injury prevention processes. Claims control and management activities can reduce the cost of a specific employee injury when it occurs. The aims of an effective claims control and management process are to:

1.   Enable the injured employee to return to work as soon as possible.

2.   Help reduce the loss, to both the employee and employer.

In order to control claims, managers and supervisors must be responsible and accountable for injuries to their employees. How an injured employee is "managed" has a dramatic effect on the end result. Managers and supervisors should treat the injured worker the same way that they would expect to be treated themselves. Reassure injured employees, let them know what is available through the company to aid their recovery, get them involved in the accident investigation as soon as possible, and let them know that work is available for them as soon as a medical professional allows them to return. A positive, caring attitude will be far more successful in limiting costs than one that is adversarial.

> Case study:
>
> Working as a heath and safety professional, I have come across almost every type of work related injury and claim. What I have found is that if you treat employees as you would like to be treated, you gain far more. The same can be said for how you treat and deal with injured or sick employees.
>
> While working as a health and safety advisor for a large blue chip business, I came across a company that provide a nationwide musculoskeletal service using local practitioners. Within this business there was a good number of employees that had previously been suffering with possible manual handling and work related upper limb disorders (WRULDs). Most of them had been waiting for some time for things like physiotherapy through the health service, on waiting lists for longer than 6 months. Having had experience of these types of injuries I knew that the majority would only need 2 or 3 treatments to make a recovery that would allow them to work with little or no restrictions.
>
> The cost of having these people off sick did almost bring these businesses' profits to their knees, with over-time, agency cover and sick pay. Within 3 weeks of using a fast track physio service for locations throughout the UK and Ireland we were able to turn this situation around, and due to the lack of time off, and the professional reports back from this service it also significantly reduced their injury claims.

A growing number of companies have specific claims management processes. It is recommended that the following sequence of activities be followed when there is an employee accident resulting in an injury:

1. At the time of the employee accident, managers should determine for themselves the severity of the injury. If the injury cannot be treated by in-house first aid, the injured employee will be taken to a medical professional, which may be their doctor, a company doctor or to hospital.

2. The company will provide transportation if possible, of the injured employee to the medical professional. This transportation may require an ambulance or taxi.

3. Once the treatment has been completed, transportation should be provided for the employee to return to the workplace or home as required.

4. When the employee returns to work a manager or supervisor should clearly assess their capabilities and what their limitations are going to be and for what length of time. Care should be taken in building up their workload.

5. The employee's manager or supervisor should meet with the individual to discuss the accident, the injury and any medical professional restrictions relating to the injury.

6. A determination should then be made as to how long the employee is going to be off work, or if they need to be off work at all, i.e. it may be possible for the individual to part take in other workplace activities and/ or development. If the case is complex and/or it appears it will involve a long period of absence, the manager or supervisor and other appropriate management personnel should be involved immediately to begin to plan a return-to-work process.

7. If the employee is to lose more than two weeks of work due to injury, the manager or supervisor and/or management representative should explain to the individual the benefits and rights as they relate to employment law, employee terms and conditions. It should be explained to the employee what their weekly income will be, when it will be received, who will be sending it to them and how it will be arranged.

8. The manager or supervisor should regularly contact the employee during the time they are off work. The aims of these contacts are to make sure the employee is receiving their benefits, to make sure that they are receiving adequate medical care, to let them feel part of the business, and to let them know they are missed. Whenever contact is made, the discussion will always include mention of when the employee will be returning to work and what will be available for them when they return. I have often been asked if this is illegal, especially when an individual has a sick note, could it not be constituted as harassment? Well most of it is about the approach of the manager or supervisor who makes contact, if you are just calling to find out if they can come into work then the answer is yes. However by following the advice above and making it a general well being call you will reduce the possibility of someone being able to make a claim of harassment.

9. A specific return-to-work process should be developed for the employee who is going to be off work for more than two weeks. It will be the manager and supervisor's responsibility to determine precisely what activities are available for the employee to perform within the possible limitations that have been set by a medical professional. This will involve

establishing a plan and, submitting the plan to the employee and possibly, the medical professional carrying out their treatment.

10. Once the return-to-work process has been accepted by all parties, a meeting will be held with the employee to discuss the details and determine what work activities will be available and when.

11. When the employee and their medical professional have agreed upon a return-to-work process, the plan can be, if needed, submitted to the insurance claims department for their information and for the termination of benefits at the agreed upon date of return to work.

12. Managers and supervisors and appropriate management personnel should monitor the workload of the employee on alternate duties. They should be certain that the employee is performing tasks within his medical limitations. Also, periodic checks should be made with the employee to determine their condition and discuss the progress toward their ultimate return to full duties.

The key to long-term success in returning employees with back injuries to work, is developing a positive open line of communication between managers, supervisors and the injured employee. If the individual genuinely feels that management cares about their well being, it is more likely that they will co-operate. A positive atmosphere is extremely important. The aim is to make the individual feel safe and welcome. Without this feeling, an employee is far more likely to seek legal advice, which will only result in higher costs and increased frustration for all.

It is important that managers and supervisors take into account that the loss of an employee also has effects on the rest of the workforce, if one person claims from a business, others are likely to follow suit with claims for similar injuries. The other important effect injured employees usually have is that the morale of the workforce decreases, not necessary straight away, but usually within a few weeks, the atmosphere in a workplace can be difficult, as people have extra pressures to make up for the person off sick.

List here what alternative duties (excluding or reducing manual handling) there are available to either, you, your role, or for those who work for you:

3.3 - Manual Handling and The Law

It used to be that manual handling concerns were around training individuals to lift heavy loads, but now manual handling legislation in most countries around the world focuses, quite rightly, on reducing injury through reducing the amount of lifting and handling a person is required to do.

My personal belief is that all over the world, health and safety laws or, in particular, those concerning manual handling, only exist for the times when money gets in the way of our morals, and that we as managers and leaders within the workplace need to do what is morally right. We will then comply with the law, as its purpose is to keep our morals in check. Think about it, do you want anyone who you work with or who works for you, to be injured?

Most legislation in Europe and internationally around the world is generally concerned with this type of module for managing manual handling activities in the workplace:

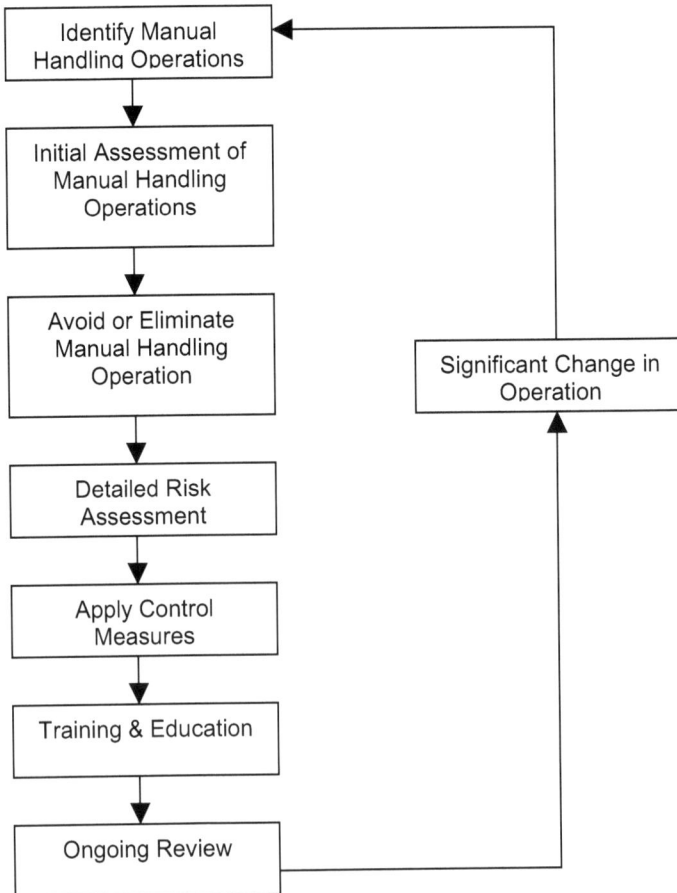

```
┌─────────────────────┐
│ Identify Manual     │◄──────────────────────┐
│ Handling Operations │                        │
└─────────┬───────────┘                        │
          ▼                                     │
┌─────────────────────┐                        │
│ Initial Assessment  │                        │
│ of Manual Handling  │                        │
│ Operations          │                        │
└─────────┬───────────┘                        │
          ▼                                     │
┌─────────────────────┐    ┌──────────────────┐│
│ Avoid or Eliminate  │    │ Significant      ││
│ Manual Handling     │    │ Change in        ││
│ Operation           │    │ Operation        ││
└─────────┬───────────┘    └────────▲─────────┘│
          ▼                         │           │
┌─────────────────────┐             │           │
│ Detailed Risk       │             │           │
│ Assessment          │             │           │
└─────────┬───────────┘             │           │
          ▼                         │           │
┌─────────────────────┐             │           │
│ Apply Control       │             │           │
│ Measures            │             │           │
└─────────┬───────────┘             │           │
          ▼                         │           │
┌─────────────────────┐             │           │
│ Training & Education│             │           │
└─────────┬───────────┘             │           │
          ▼                         │           │
┌─────────────────────┐             │           │
│ Ongoing Review      │─────────────┴───────────┘
└─────────────────────┘
```

Notes:

Notes:

Notes:

Notes:

Part 4

Reference Section

Answers to Diagrams

Figure 1.1:

    A) Cervical (neck)
    B) Thoracic (between the shoulders, where the ribs attach to the spine)
    C) Lumbar (base of the back)
    D) Sacral (back of Pelvis)
    E) Coocygeal (tail bone)

Figure 1.2:

A) Vertebra
B) Disc

Figure 1.3:

    A) Spinal Cord
    B) Nerves
    C) Herniated/Ruptured Disc
    D) Disc
    E) Vertebra

Figure 1.4:

A) Disc under pressure

Figure 1.5

A) Spine in alignment
B) Lifting using leg muscles

SUMMARY

This book provides a great deal of information about preventing back injuries and actively managing them when they occur. Managers, supervisors and employees can help in many ways including:

- ❑ Educating employees about their own back care and setting standards and procedures for them to follow.

- ❑ Supervising the use of good manual handling practices.

- ❑ Becoming involved in workplace evaluations, design and modifications.

- ❑ Encouraging teamwork and the use of mechanical lifting devices.

- ❑ Ensuring the use of correct safety clothing, such as gloves and equipment.

- ❑ Designing jobs for manual handling safety by limiting the size or weight of a load, minimising the reach and distance it has to be moved and allowing sufficient time for the activity.

- ❑ Returning injured employees to work as quickly as possible.

Become involved. It does make a difference!

Walk the Talk and lead by example

Index

ISBN 142515412-3

Printed in Great Britain
by Amazon

22477857R00057